The Midnight Court

Ciaran Carson
The Midnight Court
A new translation of
'Cúirt an Mheán Oíche'
by Brian Merriman

Wake Forest University Press

First North American edition published 2006

Printed in the United States of America
Library of Congress Catalogue Number 2005935324

ISBN (limited edition, signed and numbered cloth) 1-930630-26-3
ISBN (paperback) 1-930630-25-5

Illustrations: Untitled wood engravings (XXV and VI) from *Out of Bedlam: XXVII Wood Engravings* by Elizabeth Rivers, with texts by Christopher Smart, originally published by Dolmen Press, in Glenageary, Co. Dublin, Ireland, 1956, courtesy of James Adam & Sons Gallery

Book design by Jessica R. Koman

First published in Ireland by the Gallery Press
(Peter Fallon, Editor)

for Pádraigín Ní Uallacháin
and Len Graham

Foreword

PRECIOUS LITTLE IS KNOWN ABOUT BRIAN MERRIMAN—OR MERRYMAN, OR MAC GIOLLA MEIDHRE, AS HE IS ALTERNATIVELY KNOWN, though the latter may well be a translation from the English, rather than the other way round. Even the year of his birth is uncertain, though it is thought to be around 1745, or 1747, or 1749. His death was recorded in the *General Advertiser and Limerick Gazette* of 29th July: 'Died—on Saturday morning, in Old Clare-street, after a few hours' illness, Mr. Bryan Merryman, teacher of Mathematics, etc.' The 29th was a Monday, so Merriman died on the 27th.

John O'Donovan interviewed many old men who were 'intimately acquainted with Brian', but 'could learn no particulars about his life worth recording but that he was a stout black haired man, who held a small farm near Loch Gréine and kept a hedge school of both which he made some money, but fearing that two handsome daughters he had might be abducted from him for the sake of their little fortunes, he removed to Limerick, where he followed his old trade of teaching'. [1]

According to John O'Daly, Merriman was born and reared in the parish of Clondagad, about eight miles west of Ennis, in County Clare, and he subsequently moved to the remote and hilly parish of Feakle, where 'he composed the facetious and witty poem entitled Cúirt an mheadhon Oidhche, or Midnight Court, as fine a specimen of bardic composition as modern Gaelic ever produced, but a little licentious'.[2] O'Daly also tells us that Merriman was 'a wild youth and fond of amusement, a taste which he acquired from being an excellent performer on the violin'. But more of that anon.

---

[1] Clare Ordnance Survey Letters, 1839.

[2] Poets and Poetry of Munster, 1860.

Merriman, in later life, must also have been an excellent farmer: in 1797, seventeen years after the composition of 'Cúirt an Mheán Oíche', the Royal Dublin Society awarded him two prizes, of model spinning wheels, for his flax crop. He was also, at various periods, resident tutor with one or other of the local gentry.

What else do we know about Merriman? There is an oral tradition that he was the illegitimate son of a local squire. The theory is given some credence by the paean to bastardy which occupies a great deal of the Old Man's speech in Part Three of the poem; and there is a further suggestion that he might have been familiar with the English poet Richard Savage's composition, 'The Bastard'. For example:

Born to himself, by no possession led,
In freedom fostered, and by fortune fed;
Nor guides, nor rules his sovereign choice control,
His body independent as his soul;
Loosed to the world's wide range, enjoined no aim,
Prescribed no duty, and assigned no name:
Nature's unbounded son, he stands alone,
His heart unbiased, and his mind his own.

Another tradition has it that Merriman composed his poem during a period when he was laid up following a leg injury, whilst he was engaged to be married; and his lines on the sexual prowess of cripples, in the last part of the poem, are taken as corroboration of this speculation.

And that, more or less, is all we know of the life of the poet. But anyone who has read 'The Midnight Court' must have a picture in his or her mind as to what kind of person he might have been. For my own part, as someone who plays Irish traditional music, I was taken by the reference to his 'violin-playing'. *Violin*-playing, perhaps; and we can see him performing classical music of the day in the houses of the local gentry. But surely he must have been familiar with the music of the people: Clare, today, is an area rich in traditional music, and must have been so then. Merriman must have been a fiddle-player, and would have spent a lot of his rakish youth playing around the céilí houses of the parish. I think of the tune title, 'Hardiman the

Fiddler'—not difficult to imagine a 'Merriman the Fiddler'. And I think of the great Clare fiddle masters, such as Junior Crehan, John Kelly, Bobby Casey, P J Hayes, Patrick Kelly of Cree, Paddy Canny, and Martin Rochford of Bodyke, a few miles from Feakle: men of great subtle wit and intelligence, full of verbal as well as musical dexterity, who could not only play, but sing songs, recite, dance, tell stories and lies—'lies' being tall tales or elaborate 'wind-ups', presented with the appearance of truth, very much in the tradition of 'The Midnight Court'. I see Brian Merriman as a precursor of those men.

I had not been long reading Merriman's poem when I was struck by a strangely familiar rhythm. A jig tune, 'Larry O'Gaff' (also known as 'Daniel O'Connell' and 'Bundle and Go'), floated into my head, followed quickly by one of the songs that goes to it, 'Paddy's Panacea', which I heard from the late Tom Lenihan of Knockbrack, County Clare:

Let your quacks and newspapers be cutting their capers
'Bout curing the vapours, the scratch and the gout,
With their powders and potions, their salves and their lotions
Ochón! *in their notions, they're mighty put out.*
Would you know the true physic to bother pathetic
And pitch to the devil, cramp, colic and spleen?
You will find it, I think, if you take a big drink
With your mouth to the brink of a glass of whiskeen.

So stick to the craytur, the best thing in nature
For sinking your sorrows or raising your joys:
Oh, whack botheration, no dose in the nation
Can give consolation like whiskey, me boys. [3]

---

[3] 'The full text of the song can be found in *The Mount Callan Garland: Songs from the Repertoire of Tom Lenihan*, collected and edited by Tom Munnelly, Comhairle Béaloideas Éireann, An Coláiste Ollscoile, Baile Átha Cliath, 1994.

This measure, it seemed to me, was not such a far cry from the prosody of 'Cúirt an Mheán Oíche', with its internal rhymes and four strong beats to the line; and I decided to adopt it as a basis for my translation. The 6/8 rhythm is essentially dactylic, for the one long and two short beats of the dactyl correspond to the crochet and two quavers of the jig.[4] As the nursery rhyme has it—that fundamental rhythm to which we bounce a baby on our knee—

To market to market to buy a fat pig
Home again home again jiggedy-jig.

The nursery rhyme, the jig, and my picture of Merriman the fiddler were in my mind when, on New Year's Eve, 2004, at the entrance to St George's Market in Belfast, I was handed a religious tract by an old man. It bore a drawing of an aged fiddle-player, and featured a poem by one Myra Brooks Welch, 'The Touch of the Master's Hand', which described how a battered old violin was being auctioned for a few dollars until an old man came forward, picked up the bow, wiped the dust from the fiddle, tuned it up, and drew beautiful music from it. The bidding promptly jumped into the thousands. 'What changed its worth?' the auctioneer was asked. 'The touch of the Master's hand,' he replied. The poem concluded with a moral comparing the violin to a human soul, and the Master to God. Of course I could not help but see the Master as Merriman, who took the traditional genre of the *aisling*—or 'dream-vision', and breathed strange new life into it.

In Robert Welch's *The Oxford Companion to Irish Literature* (1996), the *aisling* is defined as 'a Gaelic literary genre, primarily associated with the political poetry of the eighteenth century, though having roots in early Irish literary texts dealing both with love and sovereignty'. Typically, 'the poet wanders forth and meets a fairy woman who is described in terms of traditional and conventional formulas; he engages in dialogue with her and asks her name, and she identifies herself as Ireland, forsaken by her legitimate spouse. The *aisling* ends with the woman declaiming a prophecy of the return of the rightful Stuart king.'

---

[4] And to the letter *D* in the Morse Code.

Merriman subverted all that. His fairy woman is not beautiful, but a threatening monster. The vision that she discloses is not of a future paradise, but a present reality. Merriman's poem, for all its rhetorical and satirical extravagance, gives us a real sense of what life must have been like in eighteenth-century Ireland: its people and their speech, their gestures, their dress, their food and drink, their recreations, and, of course, their sexual mores. The atmosphere of the 'Court' is not so much that of a court of law, but of a country market, filled with verbal commotion and colour. For all that, it is still a dream-world where Merriman can free himself from the restraints of conventional discourse, swooping from high rhetoric to street-talk in the space of a few lines—much as Dante did in the *Inferno,* which is also an *aisling.* And language is very much a concern of the *aisling:* a recurrent theme is the poet's lament for the decline of Irish, and its support mechanism of noble patronage.

I am not qualified to speak about the linguistic demographics of eighteenth-century Ireland, but the Irish language in Clare must have been on the wane even then. Merriman's language is driven towards its maximum potential, or into excess, by the fury of its protagonists. Its sometimes desperate rhetoric is always done with immense panache. Even when it lapses into logorrhoea, it questions itself. Often, Merriman, not content to say a thing once, must say it six or seven times. A classic example is the couplet, towards the end of the poem, where he plays on his own name:

Is taibhseach taitneamhach tairbheach tréitheach
Meidhreach meanmach a ainm 's is aerach.

Which means something like 'Spirited pleasant useful versatile merry mindful and lively his name'; but the effect, of near-homophones collapsing into one another, of meanings slithering into one another, is untranslatable. Let's take one word, *aerach,* which can indeed mean 'lively' or 'fond of pleasure'; but *aerach* is also 'airy', in the sense of 'volatile', and in Merriman's hands the language is indeed volatile, as its essence is pressurized, letting off steam, ever threatening to boil and vanish into thin air through its own excesses. However, the couplet is spoken not by the 'Merriman' narrator, but by the Young Woman, in a voice of contemptuous irony, so that it comes to mean the opposite of what it says. For *aerach* can also mean 'flighty', 'improvident', 'vain'. Things depend on how you say them, and who is doing the saying, and who the listening. The words, the more that you look at them, become foreign, eerie and strange: and *aerach* also means 'haunted', or 'weird'. Dinneen has the expression *áit aerach,* 'a lonely place, a place haunted by ghosts', which is the landscape in which the poem itself is set; and then we realize that the first word in the couplet, *taibhseach,* does indeed mean 'spirited'; but it also means 'ghostly'. For the protagonists of the 'Court', including 'Merriman' himself, are ghosts, summoned into being by language; they are figments of the imagination. In the 'Court' the language itself is continually interrogated, and Merriman is the great illusionist, continually spiriting words into another dimension.

What is a translator to do with all this? As soon as I began to deal with Merriman, I knew that my own grasp of Irish was not up to his manifold command. I hesitate to call myself a native speaker: true, Irish is, or was, my first language, but I learned it from parents for whom it was a second language; and it has been a long time since it was the first language in which I think, or express myself, though I sometimes dream in it. Compared with my English, my Irish is impoverished. Yet I can remember a time when English was foreign to me: a time when my father would tell me stories of the Fianna, and other heroes of ancient Ireland. I remember the landscape in which they were set; and, as I worked my way through the translation, it sometimes seemed to me that I entered that otherworld where it is always nightfall: I have been hunting, but have got separated from my companions, and I make my way through a dark wood before emerging into a mountainy region where a few lights glimmer on the hillside. These are the houses where the word-hoards are concealed.

Sometimes I would work past midnight, or lie sleepless in bed, haunted by an elusive phrase. I would get up and scribble the words down; often, when I looked at them in the morning they would crumble into dust, like jewels brought back from an enchanted realm, that cannot bear the light of this world. Marcel Proust says somewhere that a writer inhabits his native language as if it were a foreign country. For me, both languages—so familiar yet so foreign—became strange, as I wandered the borders between them. I realized my inadequacy in both. Trying to find English equivalents for Merriman's abundant lexicon of vilification, for his numerous double entendres, for the gorgeousness of his verbal music, I scoured thesauruses and dictionaries. I racked my brains. Eventually I got there.

I was helped in my journey by the constraints of rhyme, assonance and metre. I wanted to follow Merriman's couplets and quatrains as closely as possible, following in his footsteps as it were. As it happened, sometimes I transposed lines and couplets; and in some instances I departed somewhat from the 'literal' matter of Merriman's words; but I persuaded myself that even the most radical departures still bore a sidelong, metaphorical relation to the original. That is the inevitable fate of any verse translation. One is forced to look askance at the first words that enter one's mind; and seeking alternatives, with different metrical weights and different sonorities, one usually arrives at a more elegant—and, somehow, a more right—frame of words. Of course the original is changed in the process—how could it be otherwise?—but so is one's mind, one's understanding of what the words might mean; and that is how it should be. One must enter that foreign country, and learn its language anew.

On the morning of New Year's Day, 2005—the year of the two hundredth anniversary of Merriman's death—I dreamed about Merriman. I was wandering on a dark hillside when I saw a light in the distance. I followed it, and came to little house. The door was ajar; timidly, I pushed it open. Merriman was sitting by the hearth, wearing a greatcoat. He gestured at me to sit down. I did so, and we conversed. True, he did most of the talking, but I was fully able to follow the flow of his intricate Irish. I cannot remember what was said. When I awoke, I was disappointed to find my Irish restored to its former poverty. But I felt that I had been touched, just a little, by the hand of the Master.

Ciaran Carson
Feast of the Epiphany, 2005

Part One

'TWAS MY CUSTOM to stroll by a clear winding stream,
With my boots full of dew from the lush meadow green,
Near a neck of the woods where the mountain holds sway,
Without danger or fear at the dawn of the day.
The sight of Lough Graney would dazzle my eyes,
As the countryside sparkled beneath the blue skies;
Uplifting to see how the mountains were stacked,
Each head peeping over a neighbouring back.
It would lighten the heart, be it listless with age,
Enfeebled by folly, or cardiac rage—
Your wherewithal racked by financial disease—
To perceive through a gap in the wood full of trees
A squadron of ducks in a shimmering bay,
Escorting the swan on her elegant way,
The trout on the rise with its mouth to the light,
While the perch swims below like a speckledy sprite,
And the billows of blue become foam as they break
With a thunderous crash on the shores of the lake,
And the birds in the trees whistle bird-songs galore,
The deer gallop lightly through woods dark as yore,
Where trumpeting huntsmen and hounds of the hunt
Chase the shadow of Reynard, who leads from the front.

YESTERDAY morning, a cloudless blue sky
Bore the signs of another hot day in July;
Bright Phoebus arose from the darkness of night,
And got back to his business of spreading the light.
Around me were branches of trees in full leaf
And glades decked with ferns of a sylvan motif,
With flowers and herbs so profusely in train

It would banish all thoughts of despair from your brain.
Beat out as I was and in need of a doze
I laid myself down where a grassy bank rose
By the side of a ditch, in arboreal shade,
Where I stretched out my feet, and pillowed my head.
So I shut down my brain, and the lids of my eyes,
With my hat on my face to discourage the flies,
And dropped off to sleep, quite composed and serene,
When I found myself sunk in a horrible dream
That jolted my senses, and grieved my heart sore;
Lying dead to the world, I was shook to the core.

NOT LONG was my slumber when nearby, thought I,
The land rocked and rolled, and a turbulent sky
Brought a storm from the north, an incredible gale
That lit up the harbour as fire fell like hail.
In the blink of an eyelid—a thing I still see—
A female approached from the side of the quay,
Broad-arsed and big-bellied, built like a tank,
And angry as thunder from shoulder to shank.
Of her stature I made an intelligent guess
Of some twenty-one feet, while the hem of her dress
Trailed for five yards behind, through the mire and the muck,
And her mantle was slobbered with horrible guck.
Majestic and mighty to gaze on her brow,
Which was furrowed and gullied as if by a plough;
Formidable, fearsome the leer of her grin,
Purple-gummed, ulcered, with no teeth within.
Dear God! how she waved like a wand in her fist
A flagpole, so fiercely as not to be missed,
With a brazen plaque stuck to the top of a spike,
On which were inscribed a bum-bailiff's rights.

THEN GRUFFLY and roughly she uttered this spake:
Rouse yourself, stir yourself, sluggard, awake!
Shame on you, blame on you, slumped on your ear,
While the court is convened and the thousands draw near!
Not a court without standing, or statute, or code,
Nor an imported court of the plundering mode,
But a court that is ruled by a civilized throng,
Where the weak are empowered, and women are strong;
And the people of Ireland can hold their heads high
That the fairy host gathers from far and from nigh
To argue the case for two days and two nights
In the many-roomed mansion on Moygraney's heights.
And great is the grief on the mien of their king,
And his fairy assembly, ranged ring on ring,
And all of those others collectively there,
That the nation has suffered such great disrepair—
An old race indeed, without freedom or land,
Without rights to its rent, and its leaders all banned,
The rich farmlands ruined, their bounty replaced
By brambles and nettles and fields full of waste.
The nobles we had are all scattered abroad,
And upstarts and gangsters now take up the rod,
Their sport to deceive, and to rob without shame,
To exploit the blind and the halt and the lame.
O bleak is the prospect and black is the day,
When Justice lies shackled, her laws disarrayed,
The weak so enfeebled, infallibly tied
To a future of fraud where no fairness abides;
Duplicitous lawyers, and crooks on the bench,
Hush money, slush funds, and all conscience quenched,
Where backhanders buy you a piece of the judge,
And everyone knows that the law is a fudge.

ALONG with these truths—and with nothing ignored—
By an oath on the Bible that day it was sworn,
A case that is clear and you cannot refute:
That for want of its use, there's no spunk in the youth,
The numbers of weddings and offspring are down,
There's depopulation in country and town,
The land turned to desert by wave upon wave
Of masculine wars that put men in their graves,
At the whim of their leaders displaced overseas,
While no babies are made from your miserly seed.
Single and childless, you ought to feel shame
When there's women aplenty to hand on your name—
Troops of them, beautiful, young and well made,
Warm-blooded, blooming, delectable maids,
Aglow with vitality, spring in their step,
Even the languid ones oozing with pep,
And all gone to waste for the want of a woo,
With no milk in their breasts, and no fruit in their womb.
Yet give them a shake, and you'll find that they'll drop
Like overripe apples right into your lap.

AT THE CEASE of the session the wise ones decreed,
That to counter the Irish reluctance to breed,
An envoy endowed with all verbal command
Should be chosen by ballot and sent to this land.
Then Aoibheall, the truthful, who loves Munster most,
The Princess of Craglee, accepted the post,
To part from the fairy assembly that night
And travel to Thomond, to set things to right.
Beholden and noble as this lady was,
She swore to wipe out all iniquitous laws:
To stand on the side of the poor and the weak,

To ensure that the mighty become mighty meek,
That power be sheared from the powers that be,
And due right restored to its rightful degree.
I pledge now that neither imposture nor pomp,
The friendship of mistress, or madam, or pimp,
Will trample on law, as is often the case,
But acknowledge this court when Her Grace is in place.
In Feakle the hearing's about to begin,
Your summons delivered, so up on your pins;
You'll want to be off at a double-quick jog,
And no lip! or I'll drag you myself through the bog.
She hooked the lapel of my cape with her pike
And took me behind her through ditch and through dyke
At a rate of such knots that in no time at all,
We reached Moinmoy church and its white gable wall.

FLAMBOYANT in torchlight—a sight I see still—
Was a hall fitted out with professional skill,
Stately, capacious, ornate, chandeliered,
The doors well located, the seats rightly tiered.
In splendour I witnessed the Queen of the Fay
Ensconced on the bench in her legal array,
Surrounded by squadrons of guards at the ready,
Fearsome, formidable, stalwart and steady.
The seats were all taken, the people packed in
From ceiling to floor in a murmurous din.
This dream of a female then came to the fore,
Fair-haired and stately, her skin without flaw,
With eloquent gesture, her elegant hand
Held aloft as she took up her stance on the stand,
Unpinning the locks of her beautiful hair,
Which hung round her face in a show of despair,

And fiercely her piercing eyes glinted like steel,
For the quarrel behind them was hard to conceal.
Her breast heaved in spasms, confounding her speech,
So deep was her feeling, the words beyond reach,
You'd almost imagine she'd rather be dead,
So full were the floods of the tears that she shed.
Straight as an arrow she stood at the stand,
Wringing the joints of her elegant hands,
While the tide of her misery flowed down her cheek,
Till finally, sorrow allowed her to speak.
Her features unclouded, took on a new light,
And, drying her eyes, she declared what I write:

A THOUSAND times welcome, and heart-joy to thee,
O all-seeing Aoibheall, the Queen of Craglee!
O light of the day, and the moon's guarantee!
O life of the people, their hope to be free!
And, Queen of the Fay to whom honour is due,
Thomond and Ireland have dire need of you!
The cause of my sorrow, the crux of my woe,
The pain that has drained all my get-up-and-go,
That's driven me crazy, and quite round the twist,
And put me astray like a sheep in the mist,
Is the number of girls with no hope of a match,
Who in spite of their beauty remain unattached,
Made grumpy with hunger for what they can't get,
Turning into old spinsters for want of a pet.
I know for a fact that wherever I go,
There's hundreds of lassies who'd never say no:
And I am a member of that barren lot,
With no husband, no baby, and no loving knot.

I'm gutted, I'm sulky, I'm plunged in despond,
Without bounty, or household, or marital bond;
Broody and gloomy, I can't sleep at night,
Deprived of all comfort and sensual delight.
Cold is the bed where I'm tossing and turning,
My mind in a turmoil, with racy thoughts churning.

O YOUR GRACE! please consider our feminine case,
That the women of Ireland find men a disgrace,
And if things go the way that they've gone until now,
We'll have to abduct them, may God speed the plough!
When they make up their minds to combine with a wife,
You'll find that they're useless at their time of life,
When no girl in her senses would lie with such fools,
For they'll fumble the job, with no edge to their tools!
And even if Richard or Ricky or Dick,
Some fine strapping youngster with plenty of kick,
Ties up with a woman, she won't be a lass
Full of vigour and wit, or a lady with class,
Or a beauty endowed with an hourglass physique,
Or a budding young scribe of poetic mystique,
But a mangey old bag or a hatchet-faced bitch,
Who'll go to her grave undeservedly rich.

IT BUGS ME, it baits me, it makes me feel sick,
It gives me the blues and it gets on my wick,
It gives me a terrible pain in the head,
It gets up my nose and it makes me see red,
When at market or mass I would happen to spy
A well-built, intelligent, handsome young guy,
Jaunty and jolly, yet wise for his years,
Confident, charming, at ease with his peers,
Bright-eyed and bushy-tailed, up for a joke,
A go-ahead, full-blooded, good-looking bloke,
Entangled and tamed and in marriage entrapped
By a henpecking dragon, or crabbèd old yap,
Or a slut, or a slabber, a half-witted slag,
A nutcase, a hoyden, a tight-fisted hag,
A know-all, a nincompoop, full of old guff,
A stony-faced scold, never out of a huff,
And God save us all! have you just heard the news,
That one of those dirty-haired, flat-footed shrews
Will be hitched in the morning? It gives me the pip!
Why her and not me? Have the men lost their grip?
Or why have they left me to spoil on the shelf?
I'm the cream of the milk, you can see for yourself:
My mouth is enticing, my smile dazzling white,
My face is engaging, my shape is just right,
My eyes are bright green, and my curly brown hair
Has ringleted tresses and wavelets to spare;
My cheeks need no blusher or powder or puff—
The skin I was born with is still fair enough;
My hands and my throat, my fingers, my breast—
Each bit of my body competes with the rest.

And look at my waist and my elegant frame!
I'm not clumsy, or frumpy, or hunchbacked, or lame;
My bum, legs and belly all vie for attention,
And what's under cover I won't even mention.
I'm no scowling sourpuss or hussy or nark
But a handsome young filly with plenty of spark,
Not a trull nor a slut nor a fool nor a boor
Nor a throughother, ill-mannered lump of a whore,
Nor a slovenly sluggard, nor draggle-tailed ass,
But a clever young woman, the top of her class.

AND IF I were inclined—like some neighbours I know—
To be laggard and lazy, with no brains to show,
With no gumption, or savvy, or sense of what's fair,
Then what odds if you saw me fall into despair?
But at any reception, or party or spree,
At wedding or wake, of whatever degree,
At sports-field, or race-course, or on the fair green,
Where step-dancing punters in dozens are seen,
I'd be nicely turned out in an eye-catching kit,
From shoulder to hem of superlative fit,
My poll lightly powdered (too much is *de trop*),
My bonnet well starched, and adjusted just so,
The hood *à la mode*, trailing ribbons galore;
My gown of shot silk (that stuff I adore)
And its bodice befitting a well-made young maid,
Are enhanced by my cloak of the cardinal red;
There's a landscape embroidered, with branches and birds,
On my bright cambric apron, too lovely for words;
My shoes have those new-fangled, screw-in high heels
(Not the best, I'll admit, for the jigs and the reels);

I've no end of bangles and buckles and gloves,
The essential accessories every girl loves;
But look out! don't assume I'm a bashful wee chit,
A simpering ninny, a tittering twit,
A flibbertigibbet, a bird-witted geck,
A loudmouth, a mope, or a gibbering wreck.
I hold my head high in the midst of a crowd,
My gaze self-assured, and my shoulders unbowed.
At races and dances I don't hide my figure;
At parties where jorums are poured into jiggers,
At junkets and suppers and bunfights and klatches,
At Mass or at market, and big hurling matches,
I show myself off, always looking my best;
When I size up the talent, I end up depressed.

THE QUARRY eludes me, the hunt is in vain,
For men have misled me, again and again,
For all that I wooed them, with all that I had,
For all that I've suffered, they've driven me mad;
For all of the tea-leaves left after the tea,
And card-reading witches, whatever they see
In the clouds of a crystal, a new moon or old,
The casting of runes—the things I was told!—
At Shrove, Hallowe'en, or all through the year,
It meant nothing at all, that much is now clear.
Restless at nights, I would take to my bed
An apple-filled stocking for under my head;
Not a pick would I eat from one day to the next,
And the prayers I would offer would make quite a text;
I'd let my shirt drift in the bed of a stream,
In hopes that a lover might visit my dreams;

I'd sweep the yard backwards, from haystack to byre,
While hair- and nail-clippings went into the fire;
In the nook of the chimney I hung up the flail,
And under my mattress the spade was entailed;
My distaff I hid in the wheat-drying shed,
My yarn in the limekiln, no needle to thread;
I scattered my flax-seed abroad in the street,
Lay sleeping with cabbage leaves under the sheet—
Oh, I've tried all the charms, every maidenly trick,
That refer to the Fiend, and the friends of Old Nick,
But devil the one has yet brought me a man;
I'm still where I started despite all my plans.

AND THE REASON I'm pleading my case at such length,
Well, the years are beginning to drain all my strength,
Grey days are approaching, as nature dictates,
And I fear I will die in a husband-free state.
O Pearl of Paradise! with tears I invoke you!
O lighten my burden, I beg and implore you!
I beseech you! don't leave me a ne'er-to-be wife,
With no fire and no fruit to my unresolved life,
With no family, no friends, no harbour, no berth,
With a welcome in houses as cold as the earth.
By thunder and lightning! damn! and blast!
As the Queen of All Fools you'll agree I'm well cast,
When the bitches of Ireland in front of my face
Parade all their riches and brag of their taste!
When Sally got hitched, she was over the moon,
And Molly got married to some landlord's goon,
And Maggie is smothered with love from her Honey,
And daily I'm mocked by these hags with the money.

In smug satisfaction lie Shoneen and Sheila;
Busy with babies are Anne and Cecilia;
There's more of these creatures abroad than you'd credit,
While I'm on the shelf; it's the absolute limit!

TOO PATIENT too long, I'd no power to command;
I was blinded by lust, when the cure was at hand:
There are certain dried herbs of the devilish class
And magical potions you mix in a glass,
That'll get me a beau or an elegant fellow,
Who'll swoon at my feet, for they make a man mellow.
I know many girls who are into this game,
And more power to my elbow! I'll practise the same.
For doubling and coupling, an apple is good,
The peel dried and powdered, along with Monkshood;
Butterbur's useful, Heartsease as well,
Ribwort and Rue, and the Bog Asphodel,
Mistletoe, Pansy, and bold Shepherd's Purse;
With Kid's Glove and Lad's Love, a girl could do worse—
Leaves burned in secret, the heart to inflame;
And some are so secret, I can't tell their names.
You've heard of the case that had everyone baffled—
That nice-looking fellow that so-and-so snaffled?
Well, between you and me, when I asked her, she swore
She'd gone on this diet just nine months before,
Consisting of nothing but white mountain kale
And mountainy midges boiled up in brown ale.
I've run out of patience, so comfort my woe,
Or else I'll be off like a bolt from a bow.
If a cure for my pain isn't found by your court,
To rumpus or ruckus I'll have to resort!

Part Two

THEN a dirty old josser, made nimble by rage,
Jumped up in high dudgeon and took centre stage.
Contorted with anger, and bursting with pride,
His limbs were a-tremble, and fit to be tied—
Such a miserable sight in a court to be seen,
He stood in my hearing and vented his spleen:

MAY YOU ever fall deeper in danger and debt,
You ignorant slip of a blind beggar's get!
No wonder the climate has worsened of late,
And Ireland's become a calamitous state—
Our rights are in tatters, the law is an ass,
The cows without calves, and the wheat under grass.
But that's not enough, for to add to the ration,
Here's Sheila the Gig in the latest of fashion!
No wonder you're single, you grubby wee ticket,
Your clan had not even the spunk to be wicked!
Whingers and wastrels, the whole bloody lot,
What little they had has long since gone to pot!
That father of yours was a classical case
Of a freeloading bum, with no skin on his face,
No wherewithal, decency, honour, or shame,
With no grub on his table, nor good to his name,
With his unbuttoned fly showing plenty of slack,
And a rope round the waist of his dirty old mac.
If you auctioned him off, with the whole of his crew,
With his goods and his chattels and fixtures on view,
Believe me, you'd find at the end of the sale,
You'd not have the price of a good pot of ale.
And everyone's asking—it's more than mere prattle—

How brats with no income, no sheep and no cattle,
Can wear buckled shoes, and a ludicrous hat,
A handkerchief fluttering this way and that!
You might fool the world with your notions of style,
But I've seen you coming for many's the mile;
And here's the bare truth, it's an open disgrace,
That for knickers and shift you've got nothing in place,
As a pimp might discover, likewise a good breeze,
And how lovely the frills on your fine cambric sleeves!
Your waistband's a choker of cheap canvas tat,
And who knows what corsets are squeezing the fat!
For bracelets and bangles you surely don't lack,
While your mittens conceal all the blotches and hacks,
And you might tell the court on your oath, I don't think,
When you last had a dinner to wash down your drink.
You bit of bad meat, with your feet in the bog,
When you sat down to dine, did you eat with the hogs?
It's easy to say why your hair's such a sight,
When I think of the hole where you bed down at night,
With no sheet below, neither fine stuff nor coarse,
But a dirty old floor rug not fit for a horse,
With no mattress or bedclothes, or counterpane spread,
And no pillow to cradle the filth of your head,
In a festering cabin with nowhere to sit,
With swill underfoot and the air thick with soot,
The floor an allotment for all kinds of weed,
Where the track of hens' feet make an excellent screed;
The roof-tree is crooked, the gables are skew,
The thatch full of holes, and the rain pouring through.
O noble assembly! You heard how she spoke,
Parading herself in her cardinal cloak,

Preening and primping and striking a pose,
But tell me! What paid for those elegant clothes?
The ribbons, the chiffon, the frills and fandangles?
The spangles, the sequins, the bracelets and bangles?
It's hard to believe they were honestly got,
For when had you last any seed in your plot?
So how did you manage the price of a hat?
And the fancy kimono, how much was that?
I won't even mention the price of the jacket,
Or the shoes, which alone must have cost quite a packet!

O AOIBHEALL, commanding, all-powerful Queen,
I plead with you, beg you, you must intervene!
I know for a fact that the men of the nation
Are often ensnared by these pros of predation;
I know it too well, for a neighbour of mine,
A charming young fellow, to no harm inclined,
With no cares in the world, full of humour and spark,
Was inveigled by one such a feminine shark.
It sickens my happiness, seeing her strut
With her nose in the air, when I know she's a slut,
The way that she brags of her cattle and crops,
And squanders his money in all the right shops.
I happened to meet her last week in the square,
And a heftier heifer you'll not find in Clare—
Bumptious and brash with her broad-arsed physique,
And her quivering jowls, and her jaws full of cheek.
Were it not for the fact that I'm always discreet,
Not given to scandal, or talk on the street,
I could easily tell you what's known to be true,
How she'd cause a fracas, or a hullabaloo,

Stretched out in the gutter, bespattered with sick,
In a yard or a close, after turning a trick.
Her fame will precede her wherever she goes,
They'll recount her exploits in poems and prose—
With grocers and vintners in tight Ibrickane,
And farmers and drovers in broad Tirmaclane;
How the gentry and servants of Bansha and Inch,
Clarecastle, Kilbracken, and Quin proved a cinch;
With the lynch mobs of Cratloe, the thugs of Tradree,
She would often consort, and not to drink tea!

SHE WAS WICKED indeed, yet for all of her failings,
I'd find in my heart some forgiveness prevailing,
But damn her! I tell you, I saw her by day,
As towards Garus Mills I was making my way,
Sprawled out in the boreen without a stitch on,
With a bog-trotting lout going hammer and tongs.
It's a marvel, a wonder, past all comprehension,
How skilled she'd become in the art of prevention—
For all of her clinches, she kept herself thin,
And only got big when it suited her whim.
It's saying a lot for the power of the word
That no moment of grace or delay was incurred,
For no sooner had clergyman spoken the rite
Of *I join you*, with all of his clerical might,
Than her breasts spurted milk (it was more than a leak)—
Nine months to the day, if you count from last week.

O ALL you young men who are single and free,
Beware of that yoke until death guaranteed,
Where hope is deluded, and jealousy's rife,
As I learned for myself at a terrible price.
It's well known to most how I used to live life,
Before I was squeezed in the marital vice:
Ambitious, and bright, I had money to spare,
And mine was a house for good talk and fine fare;
With friends in high places, the law on my side,
My power was increased, and my fame amplified;
When I spoke people listened, and nodded their head,
For my word was my bond; in short, I was made.
My mind was at ease, I'd contentment with wealth,
Till I met a young woman who ruined my health.
Oh, a lovely wee thing, she appealed to my taste—
Good carriage and bones, and a nicely shaped waist,
A fine head of hair with a tumble of curls,
The rose in her cheek like the blush in some pearls;
Her face, when she smiled, became blooming with light;
Her whole form so kissable, made for delight,
That, head over heels, I was mad to be wed,
And dreamed every night of her warming my bed.

THERE'S NO doubt at all that I reaped what I sowed,
And for my poor judgement I paid what I owed,
For rain fell from heaven to darken my days,
In vengeance for all of my gullible ways.
The clergyman wed us, and fastened the knot,
And so I was hitched to a drunken wee sot.
I didn't demur at the bills I'd to pay

Arising from what I splurged out on that day;
And give me fair dues, I consented to treat
The unruly mob that poured in from the street,
Beggars and clergymen, all on the spree,
Delighted that victuals and drink were for free.
The candles were lit, my friends gathered round,
And many's the jorum of porter was downed,
And platefuls of chicken and ham by the score;
The music was mighty, you couldn't wish more,
And more is the pity I didn't die then
From excess of grub, or from too much champagne,
Before I lay down with the pub-crawling trull
Who turned my hair grey and who made me a fool.
Soon after the news was on everyone's lips
Of her knocking about with a bunch of bad rips;
That in bars and shebeens she would hammer the table
And stagger upstairs with whoever was able.

FOR LONG had these stories been bandied about;
I heard them as well, but I shut them all out;
And some people dared not repeat to my face
What they reckoned would drive me insane with disgrace.
And blind as I was, I refused to give in
To wink and to nod, and to titter and grin,
But the truth of the matter was plainly revealed
By the bundle of joy in her belly concealed.
'Twas no idle chatter, nor mere tittle-tattle,
Nor mischievous rumour, nor misleading prattle,
Nor some bit of moonshine you'd hear on the vine,
But a baby arriving too soon to be mine.
O stranger indeed! Such a heart-scalding fright,

To have family appear after only one night!
Baffled, bewildered, I goggled and gawked
As the bundle was swaddled, and let out a squawk,
A posset of milk set to warm by the fire,
And a bucket of cream being churned in a gyre,
And a platter of goodies well dusted with sugar,
For Marian Camley, the midwife of Crucka.
The neighbours had formed an ad hoc committee,
With nudges and whispers and slurping of tea,
And, well within earshot, I heard one remark,
O praise be to Mary, and God bless the mark,
That the nipper's the spit of his da, is he not?
Though a bit premature, the darling wee tot!
And look at the cut and the set of his limbs,
And his face, don't you see, Sal, the image of him?
The shape of his body, the form of his wrists,
And his legs and his arms and his chubby wee fists?
So they pondered the traits of the family line,
My looks, and the way that his eyes were inclined,
The shape of my nose and the bumps on his head,
My figure, my form, how he lay in the bed,
How my smile was the same, and even my laughter,
The way that I walked, and things even dafter.
But hide nor hair did I see of the pup;
For fear of the draughts, he was well swaddled up,
And the crowd in the house kept him out of my sight,
Since the air might enfeeble the darling wee mite.
I ran out of patience, and called out, Bejasus!
I'll see him right now or I'll raise a right ruckus;
I blustered and thundered, I cursed and I swore,
Till the hags of the household could take it no more,

And brought the bambino to settle me down—
And mind now, don't bruise him, don't swing him around,
He's easily upset, just a *gentle* wee rock!
And indeed, the poor girl had a terrible shock!
Don't squeeze him! Poor pet! He's had enough strife!
Don't you know he's not well, and not long for this life?
We pray that he lasts till the morning, at least;
Perhaps even now we should send for the priest!
I undid the knot of his bundle-and-go
And scanned the wee body, from noggin to toe.
Begob! Was he burly and beefy, or what?
Broad-shouldered, bouncing, his cheeks nice and fat!
Plump as a dumpling, with dimples to spare,
He'd a firm set of heels, and a fine head of hair.
His ears were well formed, and his nails were well grown;
His elbows and arms were all muscle and bone,
Wide open his nostrils and baby-blue eyes,
And already his knees were a powerful size;
Such a healthy young pup you'd be hard pushed to find,
With beauty and brawn in his body combined!

O AOIBHEALL, I shout it from pulpit and steeple!
I plead the sad case of our downtrodden people!
We're all of us trapped in a mad masquerade;
Allow us some brains, take the horns from our heads;
Abolish this law of the clerical reign,
That condemns all those fathered outside of its chains!
The birth-rate is falling, the land is devoid
Of the laughter of budding young colleens and boys;
Yet we'd raise up a nation of heroes once more
Were we free of the yoke that all people deplore!

And where is the need for extravagant sprees,
For gallons of whiskey, musicianers' fees,
And buckos sprawled out with their boots on the table,
Befuddled and boozed in a bibulous Babel,
When laid in a manger, no crib for His head,
Our Saviour was born to an unmarried maid?
The offspring of unions no clergy has blessed
Have a spring in their step, and a spark, and a zest,
For Nature herself recognizes no creed,
And she puts no restraint on our impulse to breed,
For the children of impulse are healthy and hale,
With no dimness of sight; rarely sick; never frail;
And they're quicker, more gifted, with far better heads,
Than many conceived in legitimate beds.
And the proof of my statement is ready to view,
For here, as example, is one of that crew.
D'ye see him, so gentle, so brave, and so able?
Yes, bring him right here, to the head of the table.
And take a good look; though he's only a tad,
Isn't he big for his age, and a fine strapping lad?
Such a lively wee cub, full of humour and *craic*,
With good bones to his body, and spine to his back,
No offspring of miser, or grey-bearded loon,
Or twisted old bugger, or big-bellied goon,
Or limp-wristed nancy, or greasy-palmed chancer,
But one who was got by a lusty young lancer.
It's hard to believe that a dried-up old stick,
Cooped up by his wife, with no wax to his wick,
No spark in his life, and no spunk in his veins,
No fun in his marriage, no fire in his brains,
Could sow his wild oats like an eager young stud

In the womb of a woman of passionate blood.
This youngster before you is visible proof—
For his beauty of body is hard to refute—
That he sprang like a sapling from high-powered seed,
And the coupling that made him was fiery indeed.

O QUEEN of the Heavens, you've heard my narration;
Abolish this law that's the plague of our nation!
Release from their bondage both beggar and squire;
Be they born in a mansion, or farmhouse, or byre,
Let all of our people take partners and breed
According to fancy and natural need.
Free love for us all, for young and for old!
Let the new law be written in letters of bold!
And Ireland will blossom and flower once more
With children as strong as the heroes of yore,
Like Fionn, and Cúchulainn, and all of their kind,
With no lack of courage, or presence of mind;
The dark skies will brighten, and fish crowd the seas,
The mountain will bloom in the heathery breeze;
And all of our people will give you applause,
For making us free of iniquitous laws!

Part Three

THE GIRL having listened to this peroration,
She jumped to her feet with no little impatience,
And glared at the geezer with eyes full of fire,
And gave him an earful of feminine ire:

BY THE CROWN of Craglee, if I didn't admit
That you're doting, decrepit, and feeble of wit—
And to treat this assembly with all due respect—
I'd rip off your head from its scrawny wee neck,
And I'd knock it for six with the toe of my boot,
And I'd give the remainder no end of abuse,
And I'd pluck such a tune from the strings of your heart,
I'd consign you to Hell without halo or harp.
It's beneath me to answer your cretinous case—
You snivelling creep, you're a bloody disgrace!
But I want to reveal to the court and the judge
How you made a true lady a miserable drudge.

SHE WAS POOR, and alone, without cattle or land,
With no roof, and no hearth, and no family at hand;
Bewildered by life, and as pale as a ghost,
Homeless she wandered from pillar to post,
Without respite or comfort by day and by night,
Of necessity begging the odd sup or bite.
He promised her this and he promised her that,
This wretch promised all, with his plausible chat—
Her fair share of wealth, and a field of good cows,
Her nights to be spent in a bed of soft down,
A brightly-tiled hearth, an abundance of peat,
A kitchen, a parlour, an elegant suite,

Lamb's wool and linen to weave into clothes,
And a well-slated roof on this cosy abode.
It's well known to most of the girls in the town,
That it wasn't for love that she married this clown,
But that all things being equal, 'twas better to wed
Than to walk the dark roads, and to beg for her bread.

WHAT PLEASURE she had when she got into bed
With this manky old geezer left much to be said—
Sharp were his shanks, and bony his shoulders;
Icy his thighs, and his knees even colder;
His feet bore the pong of a fire of damp turf;
His body was shrivelled, and covered in scurf.
What jewel alive could endure such a fate,
Without going as grey as her doddering mate,
Who rarely, if ever, was struck by the wish
To determine her sex, whether boy, flesh or fish?
As flaccid and bony beside her he lay—
Huffy and surly, with no urge for play.
And oh! how she longed for her conjugal right,
A jolly good tumble at least once a night.
Don't think for a minute that she was to blame,
Too modest or frigid to kindle a flame!
Attractive and bright, with an amiable heart,
This lady was skilled in the amorous art;
She'd work through the night, and she liked it a lot,
For she'd give the right fellow as good as she got,
And, urging him on with her murmurs and sighs,
She would stretch at her ease, with a gleam in her eyes.
She wouldn't retreat in a sulk at his touch,
Or assault like a wildcat, with sideswipe and scratch,

But slither and slide in a mutual embrace,
Her legs round his body, her face to his face,
Exchanging sweet nothings, and stroking his skin,
Her mouth on his mouth, and their tongues going in,
Caressing his back with the ball of her heel,
And rubbing her brush from his waist to his knee.
As for the old sluggard, she'd snatch off the quilt
And try to arouse what lay under his kilt,
But for all that she nuzzled and nibbled and squeezed,
The more that she snuggled, and tickled and teased—
Well, I hate to relate how she spent the whole night,
Despairingly wrapped in her amorous plight;
Tossing and turning with bedclothes awry,
She'd shiver and shake till she thought she would die,
From sunset to dawn neither waking nor sleeping,
But hugging her bosom, and sobbing and weeping.

HOW DARE this old dirt-bird discuss womankind,
When a proof of his manhood no woman can find!
And were he a blade who'd got no satisfaction,
I might go along with his angry reaction.
Take a fox on the prowl, or a fish in the mere,
An eagle on wing or a wandering deer—
Would any dumb beast, for a day or a year,
Go hungry for grub when its lunch is so near?
And where in the world would you find such a case,
Of a brute so perverse, with a brain so debased,
That it grazed stony pastures, or fields of bare clay,
When under its nose was a fine feed of hay?
Answer me now, you despicable leech,
And I'll fathom the depths of your floundering speech!

When you sit down to dinner, what matter to you,
If the lady's been feasting for one month or two?
Would your acre of spuds be less likely to yield,
If five million Playboys had ploughed the same field?
Do you breathe? Do you feel? Do you shrink at a touch?
Do you think you might want if you want it too much?
And how many gulps do you think it might take,
To empty the Shannon, and drain all its lakes?
How many cupfuls to bail out the ocean?
How deep down its bed, do you have any notion?
Now, don't be so headstrong, the next time you chat;
As for the two horns, keep them under your hat.
And don't throw a fit, or fall out of your tree
At the thought of a girl who is easy and free;
If she spent the day serving a jolly fine crew,
There still would be plenty left over for you.
Bejasus! such jealousy might be allowed
In a stud of some standing, a man well endowed
With panache and pizzazz, full of gusto and go,
With good shots in his locker, and strings to his bow—
A rollicking rover, a noble explorer,
A foraging forward, a dashing top scorer—
But not in a doddering, cack-handed clod,
A grumpy old runt with no bone in his rod!

IT'S TIME that I mentioned a puzzle I've pondered,
A thorny conundrum that fills me with wonder—
Why priests when ordained in the clerical life
Are enjoined not to join or engage with a wife.
I chafe and I fret, like a bird in a cage;
Great is the patience that tempers my rage
That given the number of girls without men,
From the fellows in black we are forced to abstain.
O pity the maid of an amorous bent,
When she sees such a rosy-cheeked clerical gent,
Of classic proportions, handsome and tall,
Broad-shouldered, slim-waisted, bum nice and small,
Fresh-faced and smiling, his muscles well toned,
In the bloom of his youth, with firm flesh on his bones,
Solidly built, with an upstanding back,
Well able for pleasure, and up for the *craic*.
At the highest of tables they're welcome to dine,
With Waterford crystal, the finest of wine;
Downy their pillows, and ample their beds;
Provided with dainties, they're always well fed,
Most of them young, with their spunk at full flood,
For as we girls can tell you, they're real flesh and blood.
Were they tittering pansies, or poxy old gets,
Or young whippersnappers, I'd not be upset,
But they're sporty young fellows with shot in their guns,
Asleep on the job when there's work to be done!

AND SOME, I believe, might well chance their arm
For a wee bit of fun, and if so, what's the harm?
There's good and there's bad, and to give them their due,
You don't hang the many because of the few,
And to blame the whole order, it just wouldn't do;
You don't sink the ship to drown one of the crew.
Now some, it's well known, have always been rakes,
And others have broken what rules they could break,
And there's cranky old buggers—they're not hard to find—
Full of ranting and raving, who hate womankind.
But others unlike them are kindly disposed,
And are touched by the love from which charity flows:
And many's the girl who had set out her stall
Found it heaving with goods, from a clerical call.
It's well I remember their members being praised
For the wonderful families their efforts have raised;
It's often I've heard through the breadth of the land,
Appreciative words for their principled stand;
It's often I've seen the results of their labours
Being given false names, and brought up by the neighbours.
But it sickens my heart, when they spend all their time
With widows and wives who are well past their prime,
While the maidens of Ireland cry out in their need—
Such a terrible waste of the sanctified seed!
Such woe that is caused to the whole of the nation,
By clerical orders of no propagation!
O Kernel of Knowledge, I want to submit
That the celibate state is a baneful remit,
And that most who endure it have entered it blind.
And if blind I might be, draw the veil from my mind,

Recite, as you can, what the Prophets affirmed,
That same teaching of love the Apostle confirmed—
For where is it written, by what Word Divine,
That the joys of the flesh should in jail be confined?
I don't think St Paul ever said to a soul
Not to marry, but told us to go out and sow,
To part from our parents, and cleave to a wife,
Two bodies as close as the haft to the knife.
I know it's presumptuous of me, a mere girl
To quote scripture to you, O Heavenly Pearl!
For Your Grace can remember the Biblical text,
Every twist, every turn, from each word to the next,
Every pith, every gist, every meaning unfold,
Of the stories that Christ to the multitudes told:
God's Mother Herself was espoused to a man,
And Woman is big in the Biblical plan.

I BEG and implore you, O All-knowing Vision!
Descended from heaven, give us a decision!
O Glorious Light! O Queen of the Nation!
Incline to my pleading, and further our station;
Weigh in your mind all our feminine needs,
The thousands of fields without husband or seed,
For the number of females is on the increase,
Falling over each other like flocks of young geese.
And the urchins you see running wild on the street—
Skinny wee lassies with dirty wee feet—
Will be healthy and fat in a month and a day
Should you feed them with greens and big mugfuls of whey,
Till they put on a spurt of unstoppable force,
And they blossom and bud as their blood takes its course.

It sickens my happiness! Look for a mate?
When I have to contend with a river in spate?
Hope for a tumble, a wee bit of fun,
When the girls are outnumbered by men three to one?
The province of Munster is utterly sunk,
And the wastrels of Munster are wasting their spunk;
The weeds are increasing, the country is spent,
Its youth growing feeble and agèd and bent.
Unmarried, impatient, deprived of coition,
I'm looking to you to improve my position:
So get me a man, and like birds of a feather
We'll make a fine couplet in harness together!

Part Four

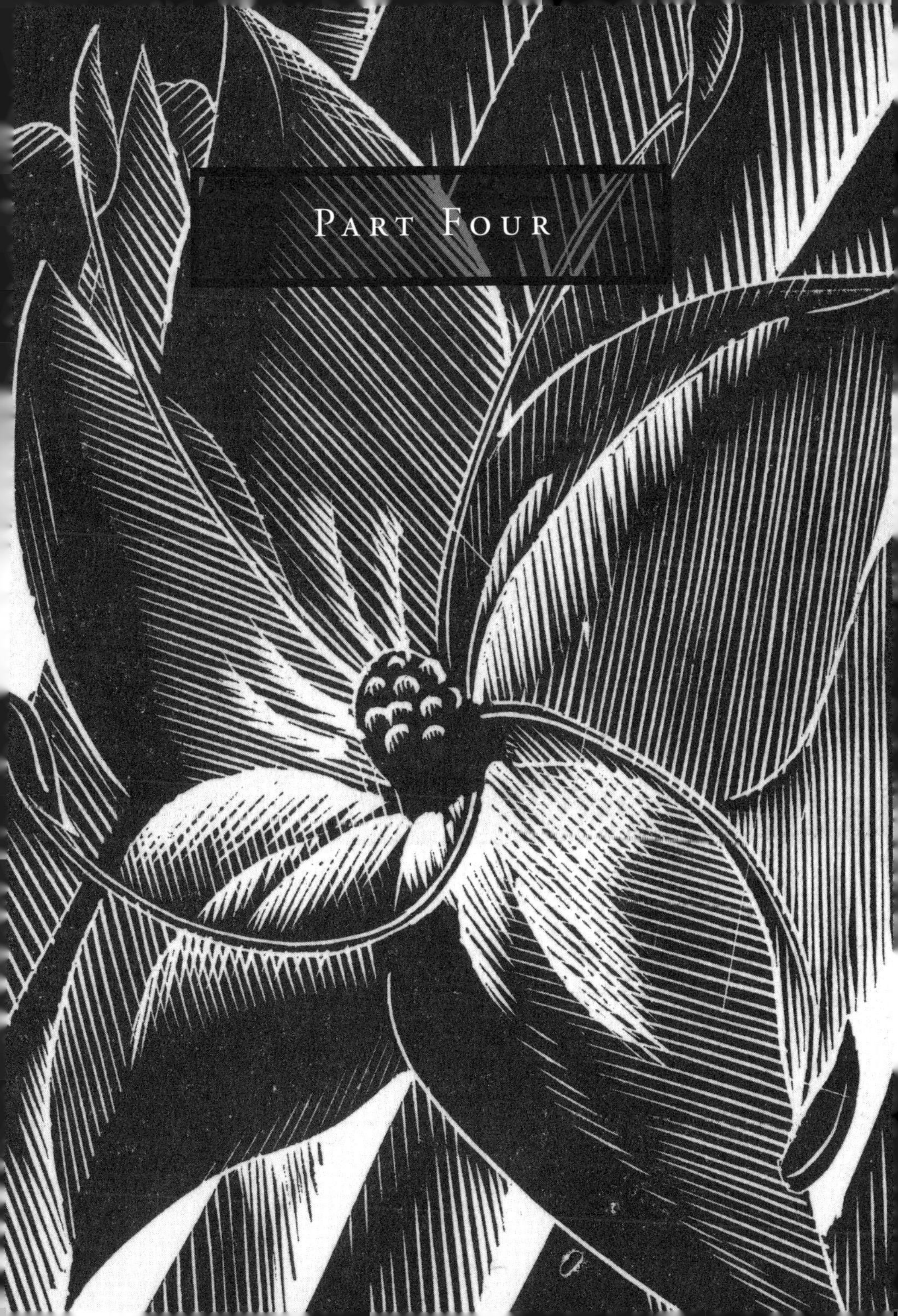

AT THE HEAD of the bench rose the stately maiden;
Day was a-dawning, and darkness fading;
Lissome and lovely her form and her face,
Tuneful her voice, full of beauty and grace.
Clenching her fists, with imperious cadence
She ordered the bailiff to motion for silence—
A hush in the court as the judgement was made,
Her words pouring forth in a measured cascade:

I FIND I'm persuaded by all you have said,
And your language well chosen, O unhappy maid!
It's clear to me now, and a matter most grave
That the offspring of Orla, and Mór, and of Medbh,
Are con men and shysters, and phonies and fakes,
Connivers, contrivers, and poxy old rakes,
The dregs of the barrel, the scum at the top,
All fighting like mad for control of the shop.
I therefore establish these laws for your state:
If he's one year and twenty, and still has no mate,
The man shall be dragged by the hair of his head
And hitched to the tree by the graveyard instead;
Of his coat and his shirt he'll be forcibly stripped,
And his back shall be flayed with a whopping great whip.
As for all those old gits, who invariably failed
To avail of the service of Mickey the Nail,
To pleasure a woman when they were well able
To raise a magnificent Tower of Babel,
Who wasted their seed at the height of their powers,
And never once plucked from the field full of flowers—
What torture they merit I leave up to you,

O ladies whose vengeance is long overdue!
Hammer and tongs, perhaps, heated red-hot—
But I'm sure that you girls can do better than that,
So debate with yourselves, decide how to act,
And I'll furnish the force to make fiction a fact—
Unlimited powers to punish at will,
And I don't mind at all if you maim, wound, or kill.

I DON'T mind at all how you treat the old ancients—
Doddery, toothless, annoying my patience,
No force in their fork, and no spuds to their root,
Drooling and drooping, producing no fruit.
But let the young people begin the begetting,
And maybe they'd make for a good family setting.
For often I've witnessed a useless old fellow
Attached to a household, hard done by, yet mellow,
Excusing the wife when she's out on the tear,
Quite happy to have all the kids in his care,
To give them his name, though he's sure they're not his—
And of this I approve, if that's how it is.

A RUMOUR I heard, that I put to one side,
For the gab of old women I cannot abide;
So it's button your lip, keep your eye on the ball,
And whatever you say, say nothing at all!
But beware of the wiles of the powers that be,
For the word is the clergy will marry, you'll see!
And committees in Rome will approve a decree,
Which the Pope will endorse with the seal of the See:
That given the desperate state of the nation,
Priests should combine against depopulation—

Lusty big fellows, with plenty of kick,
Who'll do as you please, and you'll each have your pick.
As for men far too long to the apron-strings tied,
Just read them my Riot Act—you'll be surprised!
And by the same token, don't suffer old fools—
Women in britches, or ignorant tools—
But hunt the old buggers o'er hedges and ditches
And rid the whole country of such sons of bitches.

THE TIME has now come that I must be away;
I have matters in hand that will brook no delay;
Through Munster I travel both early and late,
And what business I have here will just have to wait.
But I'll be back! And some men will quake in their boots—
Blackguards and braggarts, unscrupulous brutes,
Whose thoughts, when they have them, are nothing but base,
Who trumpet their exploits all over the place,
How this one was easy, and that one a minx,
While everyone sees through their nudges and winks—
Fine fellows indeed, whose idea of fun
Is to slander the sex, when they might have had none,
For it's not out of lust that they shoot off their mouths,
By animal spirits or passion aroused,
Nor the throb in the veins of the furious lad,
But to bandy their names as accomplished young cads;
And no pleasure drives them, but pleasure in lies,
As they bluster and bawl of performance and size,
And giggle and honk like the geese in the bog,
When in fact you could squeeze out more spunk from a frog;
And for all that they brag of their puppy dog's tail,
If it's touched by a woman, it shrinks like a snail.

I'd deal with these sluggards right now if I could,
But time is too short, and appointments intrude.
I'll tie up the buggers in shackles and chains,
Until the next month, when I'll be back again.

I'D LISTENED intently to Aoibheall's critique,
And my heart gave a lurch when she finished her speech;
A shudder came over my body and mind,
My senses with tumult and torpor combined;
It seemed that the courtroom was coming down round me,
As quaking and shaking her utterance found me.
The bailiff rose up in the name of the law;
I went pale as she stretched out her horrible paw,
And, seizing my ear with implacable rage,
Triumphantly dragged me to take centre stage.
Then up jumped the lassie who'd never say no,
With fire in her eyes and her cheeks all aglow,
And cried out with venom:

You crusty old quill!
I've longed for the day you'd be put on to grill!
You often were prompted, you tight-fisted git,
To succumb to the laws of this feminine writ—
Now who will speak up for your miserable cause?
You deserve not a word, you flabby old cod!
Where is the proof of your amorous labours?
Where are the ladies who relished your favours?
Inspect all his members, O Heavenly Princess—
No blemish I see that would render him useless.
Scan him all over, and don't be discreet,
From his baldy old head to the soles of his feet.
He's human, all right, though he looks like an ape,

But with all the right bits, of a tolerable shape.
A bit pale for me, though! I prefer tanned,
And he's not a bad height, if you get him to stand.
Fair enough, he might have a hump on his back,
But hunchbacks are often quite good in the sack,
And a gimp is the boy when he handles a lance,
And if both legs are bad, there'll be one that can dance!
And speaking of crooked, I think there's a plan
To keep this creep single, let's call him a man.
It seems he's well thought of by all of the gentry:
To all of their soirées he's given free entry,
Invited to hobnob by big blazing fires,
For his grand conversations are widely admired,
And with squireen and buckeen he likes to collogue—
The slimeball! I almost was fooled by this rogue,
Who thinks himself droll, and a fiddler of fame,
A man who is Merry by nature and name!
Such a natural freak, though, you couldn't make up,
A decrepit old ram that still has to tup!
You gibbering twit, your comeuppance is nigh,
And your bullshit won't save you, so don't even try!
For the lines of your crime are inscribed on your face—
Thirty odd years, with no marriage in place.

THEN HEAR my complaint, O Princess of Patience,
And help me determine the length of his sentence:
The torment and sorrow that smothered my joy,
That I want to take out on this crooked old boy.
Give me a hand, girls! And catch the old clown!
Una, the rope! Someone else, hold him down!
Anne, shake a leg! You can do better surely!

And Eve, grab his hands, and tie them securely!
And Molly and Mary, and Kathleen and Clare,
Let's spring into action, and yes, strip him bare!
Let's follow the words of her law to the letter;
Leave marks on his flesh, the deeper the better;
Don't stint in your efforts, and take out your stress
On the backside of Brian, who's earned nothing less,
And more power to the whip, as you lift your hands high!
He's a perfect old scapegoat, the plum in the pie,
So apply yourselves freely to legs, back, and bum,
Cut him deep, cut him dearly, and let the blood come!
Let the crack of the horsewhip resound through the land,
To flutter the hearts of the bachelor band!
So correct are the rules of this statute, I think,
That the date of the act should be written in ink.
Now here's a conundrum: eleven times ten
Subtract from one thousand, and twice what you've then
Will leave you with seventeen hundred and eighty,
The year that we ponder these matters so weighty.

I SHIVERED and shook, as she took up the pen,
For fear of the whip, not to mention the pain,
And the moment she sat down to set the date down,
With bailiff and sentinels gathered around,
I woke from my dream of the powers that be;
I sprang from my sleep in one bound, and was free!

Acknowledgements

I AM FIRST OF ALL MOST GRATEFUL to the Committee of Cúirt Festival, Galway, whose idea it was to commission this work. I would not have thought of it otherwise. The support and financial assistance of Cumann Merriman is also gratefully acknowledged.

DURING THE PROCESS OF TRANSLATION I consulted other translations, including those of Frank O'Connor, David Marcus, Patrick C. Power, and Noel Fahey's web translation at http://www.showhouse.com/welcome.html. Some phrases and rhymes in my translation have been inspired by theirs.

I TOOK AS MY BASIC TEXT *Cúirt an Mheon-Oíche*, edited by Liam P. Ó Murchú, An Clóchomhar Tta, 1982. However, on occasions my translation was influenced by alternative readings as given by Patrick C. Power in his parallel text.

THE DETAILS OF MERRIMAN'S LIFE in my Preface were gleaned from Liam P. Ó Murchú and Noel Fahey.